CogAT ®
Practice Workbook
Form 7, Level 7
(Grade 1)

© Redmond Ridge Montessori

Copyright 2020 © Redmond Ridge Montessori

Written and Edited by Gifted Test Prep Team, led by Manjari Gupta, Redmond Ridge Montessori, Redmond Washington.

All rights reserved. This book or any portions thereof may not be reproduced or reused in any manner whatsoever without the written permission of Sunshine Education LLC.

Email: info@redmondridgemontessori.com

The CogAT® is a registered trademark of Houghton Mifflin Harcourt. The test publisher does not endorse this product.

Table Of Contents

Section 1: Verbal
- Picture Analogies 5
- Picture Classification 11
- Sentence Completion 19

Section 2: Non-Verbal
- Figure Analogies 27
- Figure Classification 33
- Paper Folding 41

Section 3: Quantitative
- Number Analogies 48
- Number Series 54
- Number Puzzles 62

Answer Key 69

Section 1: Verbal | Picture Analogies

In a 2×2 matrix with 3 pictures and 1 empty cell. Students are required to examine the relationship between the top 2 pictures. From the options given color the bubble under the picture that shows the same relationship as the top two pictures.

 1.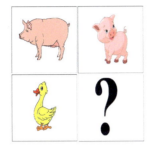
    ○   ○   ○   ○

 2.
    ○   ○   ○   ○

---

3.    5
   ○   ○   ○   ○

© Redmond Ridge Montessori

Picture Analogies

 4.
　　　　　　　　　　　　○　　　○　　　○　　　○

 5.
　　　　　　　　　　　　○　　　○　　　○　　　○

 6.
　　　　　　　　　　　　○　　　○　　　○　　　○

© Redmond Ridge Montessori

Picture Analogies

7.

8.

9.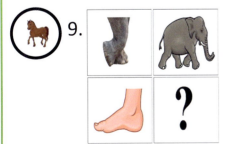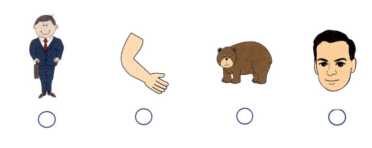

Picture Analogies

 10.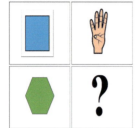

11.

○   ○   ○   ○

12.

© Redmond Ridge Montessori

Picture Analogies

13.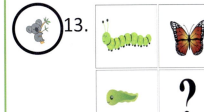

14.

15.

© Redmond Ridge Montessori

Picture Analogies

16.

_____

Section 1: Verbal | Picture Classification

Students are required to look at the top 3 pictures and examine how they are grouped together. From the options given color the bubble under the picture that is most similar to the top three pictures.

 1.

   ○

 2.

○ ○ ○ ○

© Redmond Ridge Montessori

Picture Classification

 3.

 4.

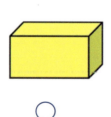   

© Redmond Ridge Montessori

Picture Classification

 5.

 ○   ○   ○   ○

 6.

O U A

f B 7 I
○ ○ ○ ○

© Redmond Ridge Montessori 13

Picture Classification

 7.

○ ○ ○ ○

 8.

○ ○ ○ ○

© Redmond Ridge Montessori

Picture Classification

 9.

 10.

© Redmond Ridge Montessori

Picture Classification

 11.

○   ○   ○   ○

_____

 12.   8   2   6

   7 
○   ○   ○   ○

© Redmond Ridge MONTESSORI   16

Picture Classification

 13.

 14.

Picture Classification

 15.

○ ○ ○ ○

 16.

○ ○ ○ ○

© Redmond Ridge Montessori

Section 1: Verbal | Sentence Completion

Students are required to listen to the question and answer it by coloring the bubble under the picture that answers that question. The question is not written on the paper in the actual test. The proctor will read the question only once.

 1. Nena's mom went to a grocery store and picked a dozen of something. Which one of these shows a dozen?

_____

2. Layla went shopping with her mom and she bought an eraser that costs a Nickel. Which one of these shows a Nickle?

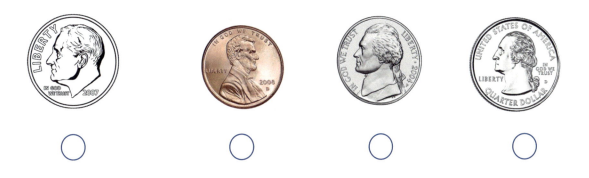

© Redmond Ridge Montessori

Sentence Completion

3. If you want to ride on a roller coaster you have to be at least 40 pounds. Which one of these you will use to find out if you are allowed on the ride?

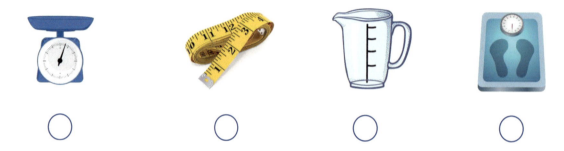

○   ○   ○   ○

_____

4. Mr. Chuck asked Eva to get something which is shaped like a sphere. Which one do you think Eva got?

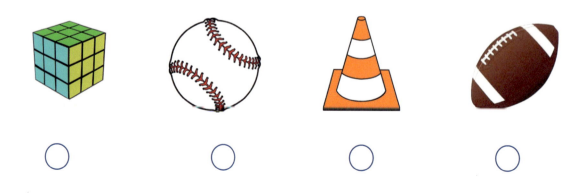

○   ○   ○   ○

© Redmond Ridge Montessori

Sentence Completion

 5. Brandon was feeling sick. Which one of these should he see?

_____

 6. It was pouring heavily, and Misha wanted to measure the rain. Which instrument did she use to measure rain?

Sentence Completion

 7. Which one of these is ancient?

_____

 8. Which one of these is the flag of USA?

Sentence Completion

 9. Grace went on a trip with her family. She visited a famous monument there. Which one of these did she visit?

---

 10. Which one of these shows a litter?

Sentence Completion

 11. If you are in Antarctica, which one of these will you probably see?

_____

 12. Sam's dad is a chef. Which picture shows Sam's dad at work?

© Redmond Ridge Montessori

Sentence Completion

 13. Which of these grow on a vine?

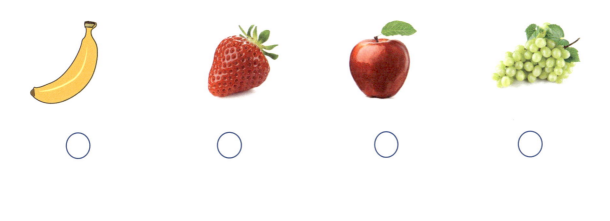

_____

14. Zoe went to a museum to see something that is extinct. Which one of these did Zoe go to see in the museum?

Sentence Completion

 15. Lila's mom is baking a cake. She wants to measure 2 cups of flour for the recipe. Which one of these would she use?

_____

 16. Which one of these does not belong in a farm?

Section 2: Non - Verbal | Figure Analogies

In a 2×2 matrix with 3 pictures and 1 empty cell. Students are required to examine the relationship between the top 2 pictures. From the options given color the bubble under the picture that shows the same relationship as the top two pictures.

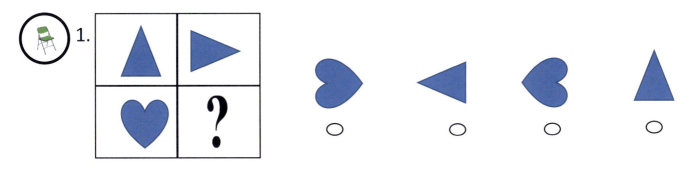

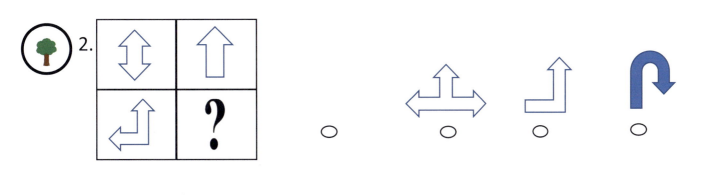

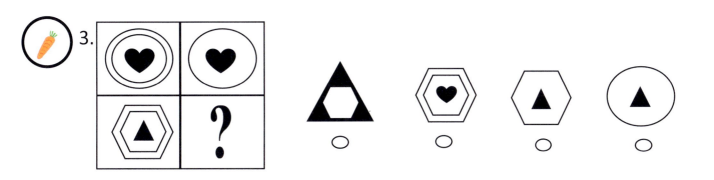

© Redmond Ridge Montessori

Figure Analogies

4.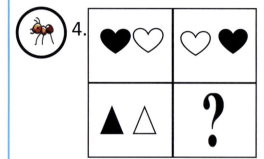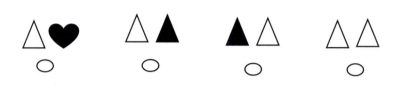

5.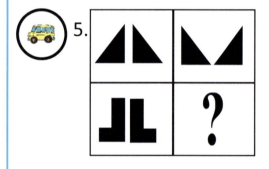

6.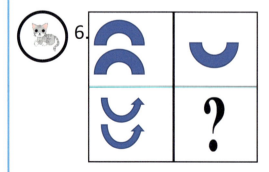

© Redmond Ridge Montessori

Figure Analogies

7.
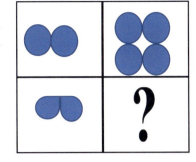

8.
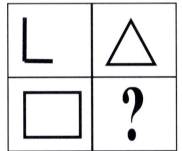 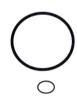

9.
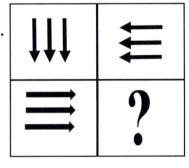

© Redmond Ridge Montessori

Figure Analogies

10.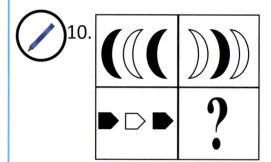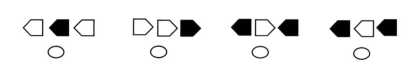

11.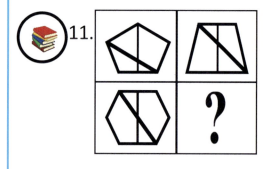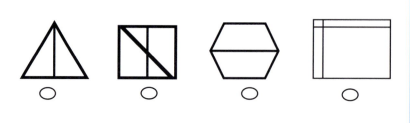

12.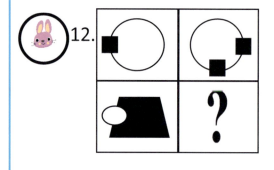

Figure Analogies

13.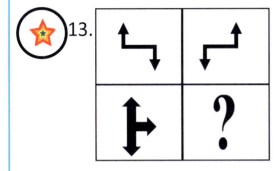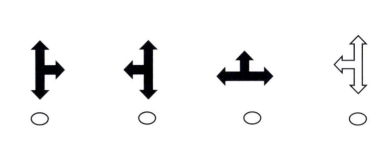

14.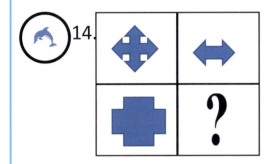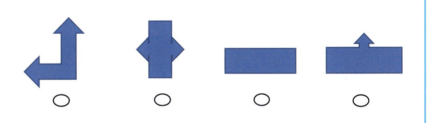

15.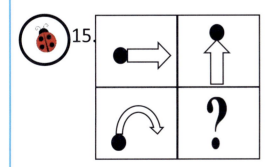

Figure Analogies

16.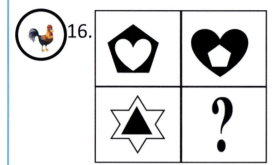

Section 2: Non - Verbal | Figure Classification

Students are required to look at the top 3 pictures and examine how they are grouped together. From the options given color the bubble under the picture that is most similar to the top three pictures.

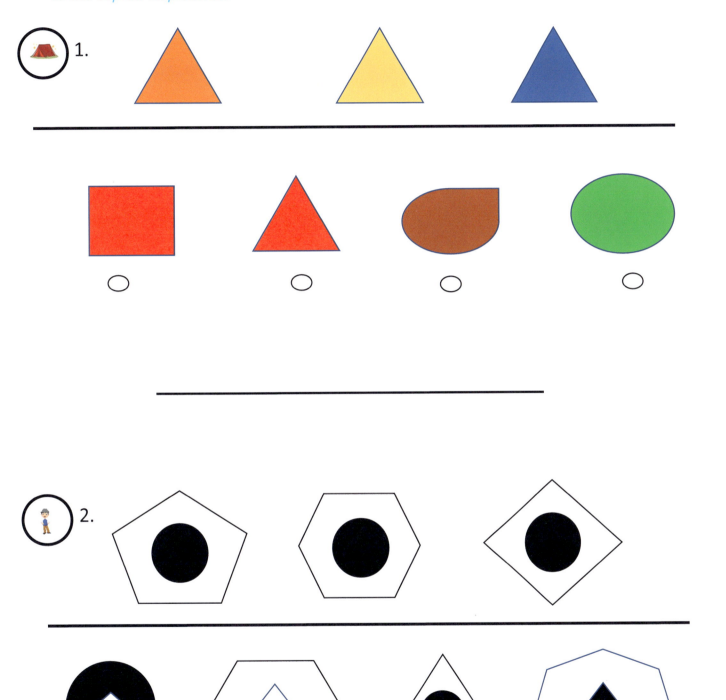

Figure Classification

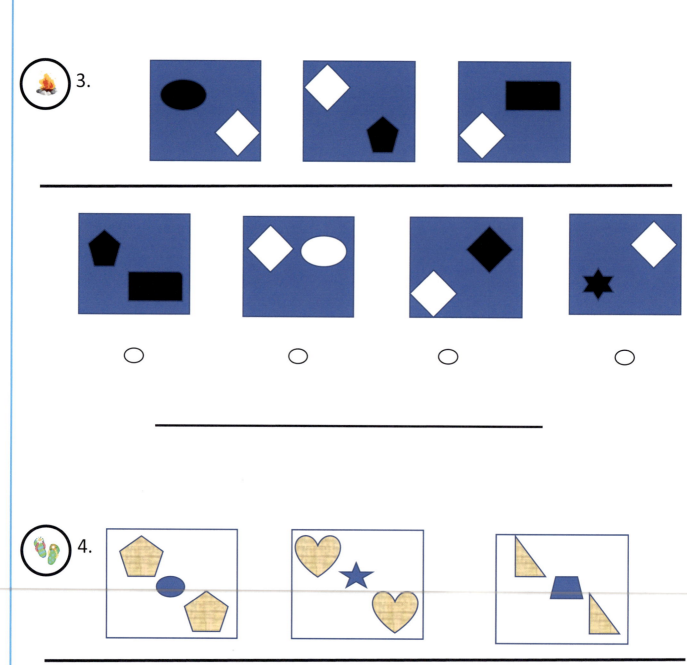

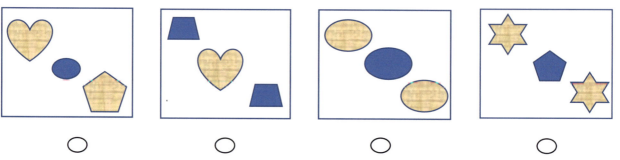

Figure Classification

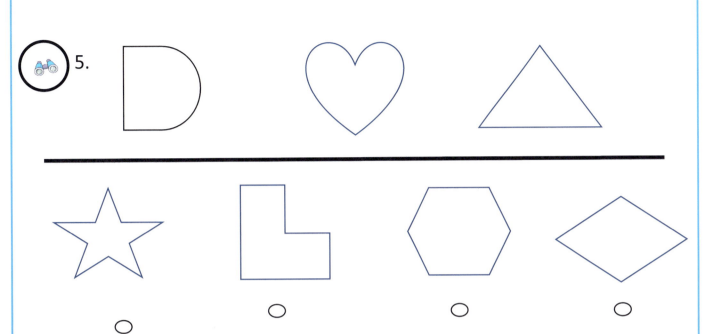

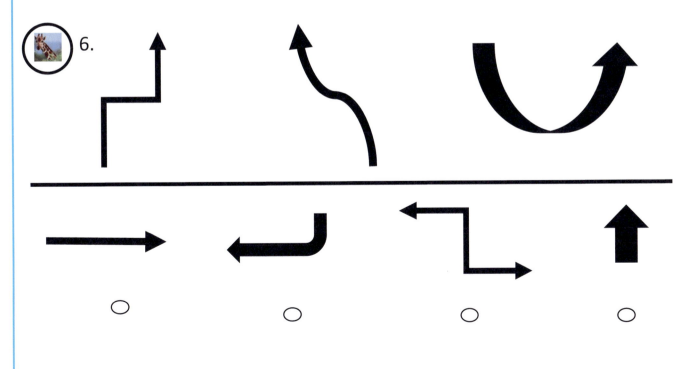

Figure Classification

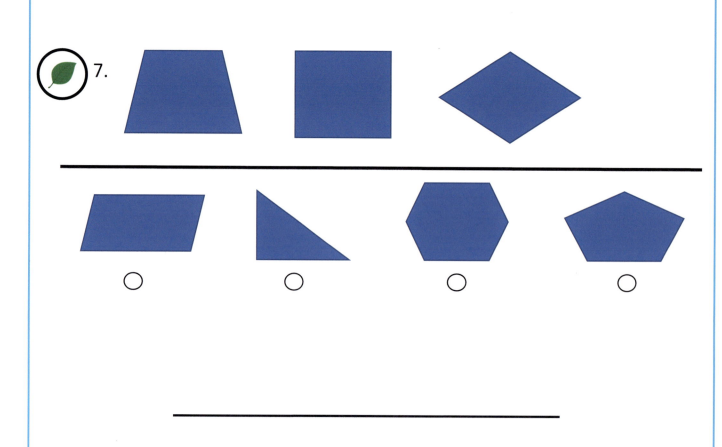

7.

8.

 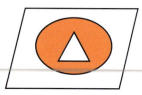  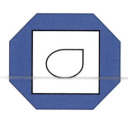

© Redmond Ridge Montessori

36

Figure Classification

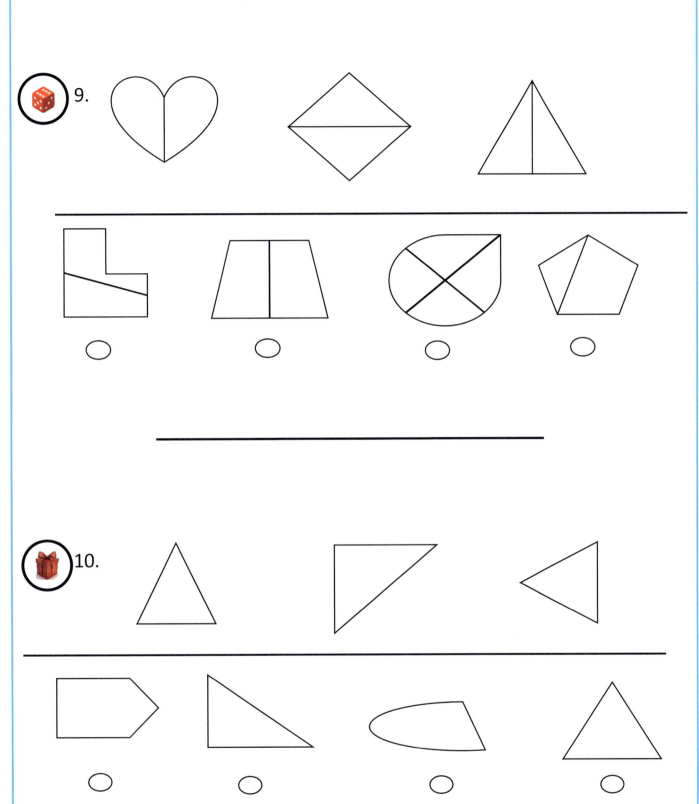

Figure Classification

11.

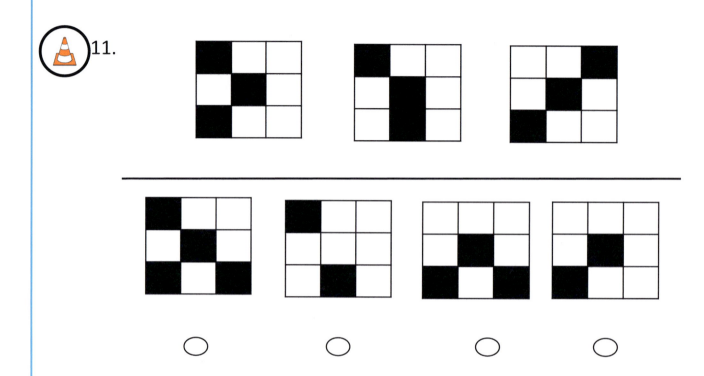

12.

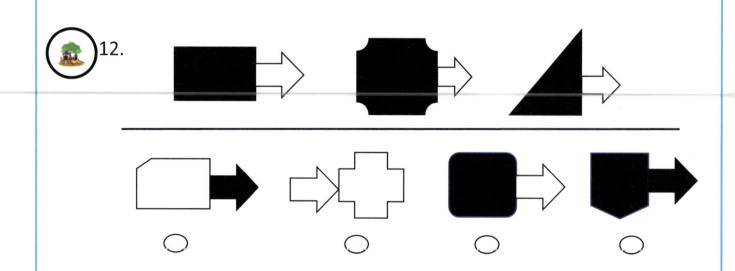

Figure Classification

 13.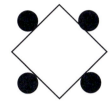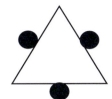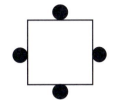

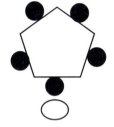  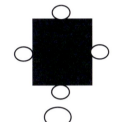 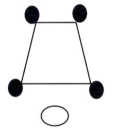

 14.

Figure Classification

 15.

 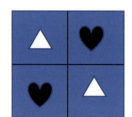 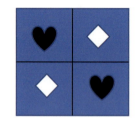

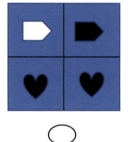 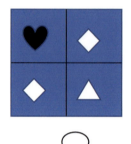 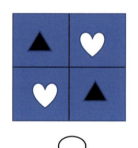 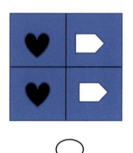
○ ○ ○ ○

 16.

   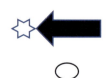
○ ○ ○ ○

© Redmond Ridge Montessori

Section 2: Non - Verbal | Paper Folding

The student is shown how a square piece of dark paper is folded and where holes are punched in it. The student is to figure out how the paper will look when it is unfolded.

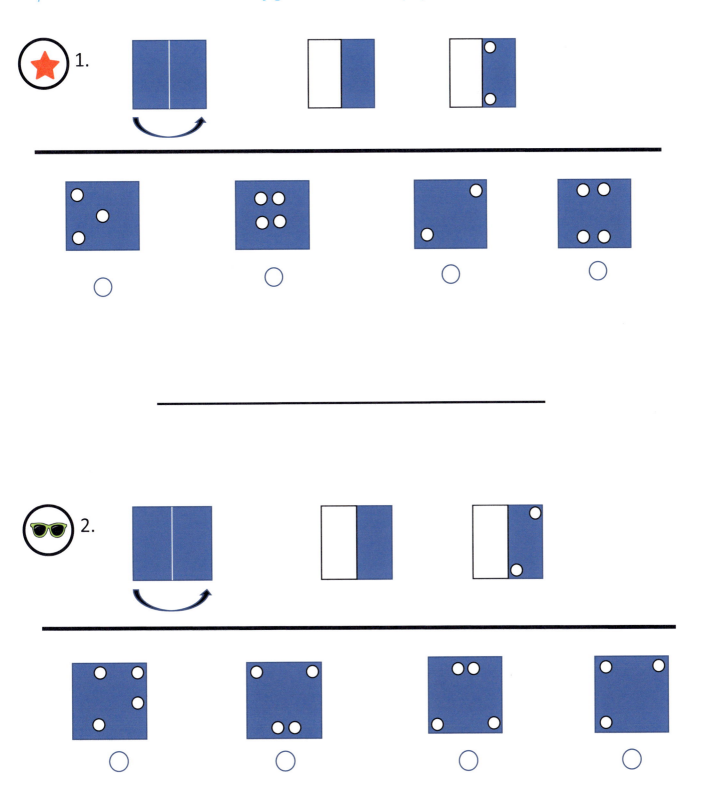

Paper Folding

 3.

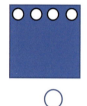  
○ ○ ○ ○

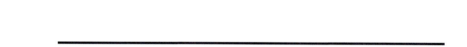

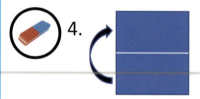 4.

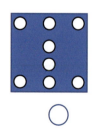 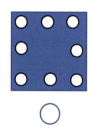 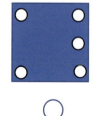 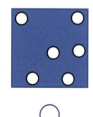
○ ○ ○ ○

Paper Folding

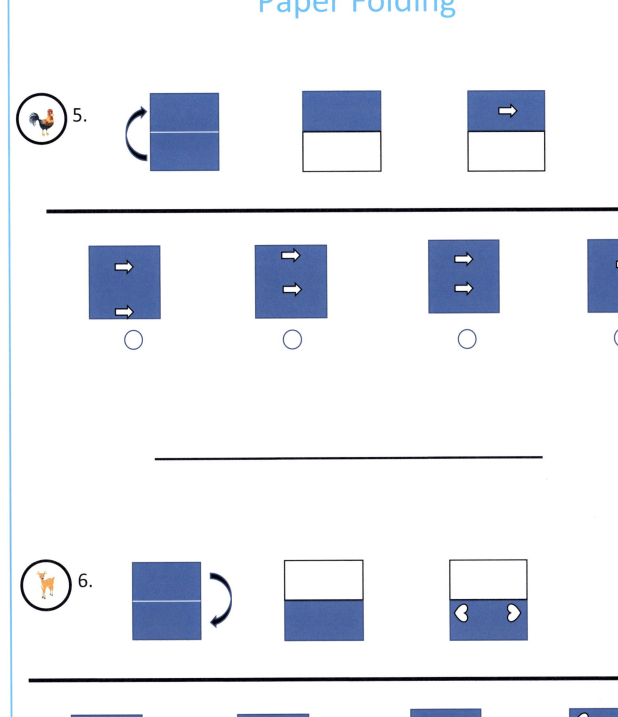

Paper Folding

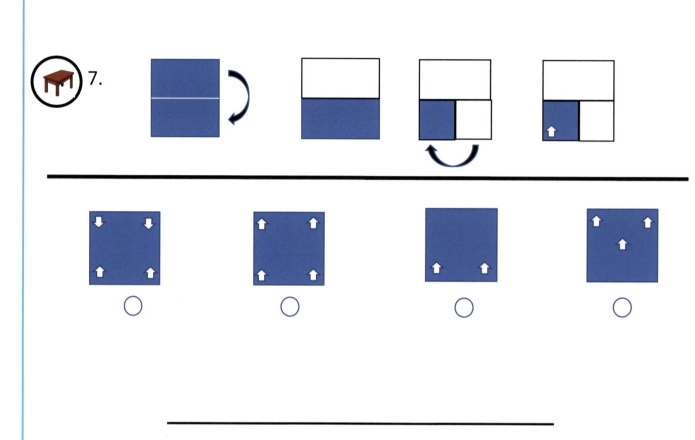

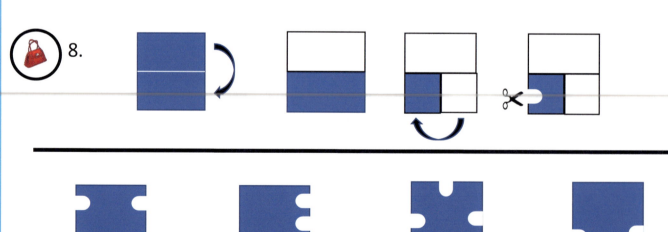

Paper Folding

 9.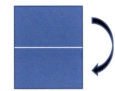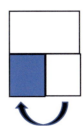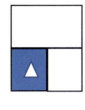

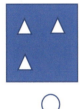   

 10.

Paper Folding

 11.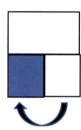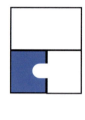

○ ○ ○ ○

 12.

○ ○ ○ ○

© Redmond Ridge Montessori

Paper Folding

 13.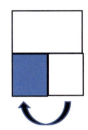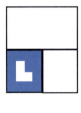

○ ○ ○ ○

 14.

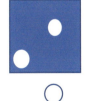 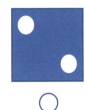
○ ○ ○ ○

Section 3: Quantitative | Number Analogies

In a 2×2 matrix with 3 pictures and 1 empty cell. Students are required to examine the relationship between the top 2 pictures. From the options given color the bubble under the picture that shows the same relationship as the top two pictures.

1.

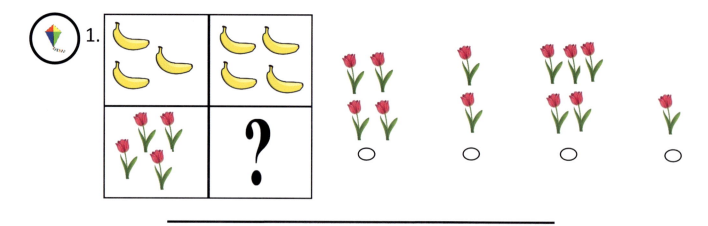

2.

3.

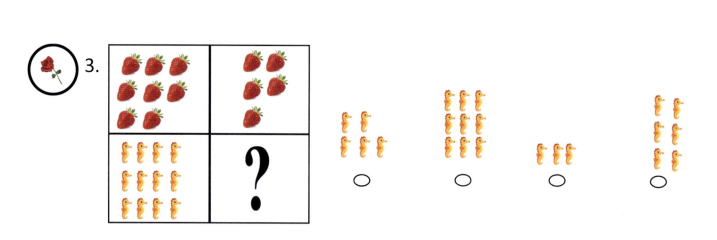

© Redmond Ridge Montessori

48

Number Analogies

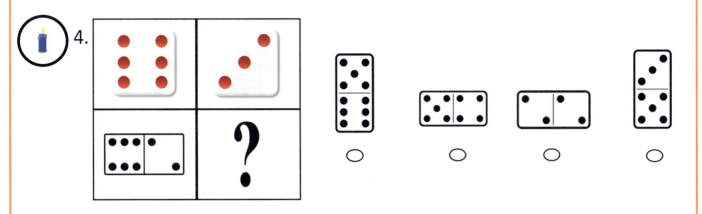

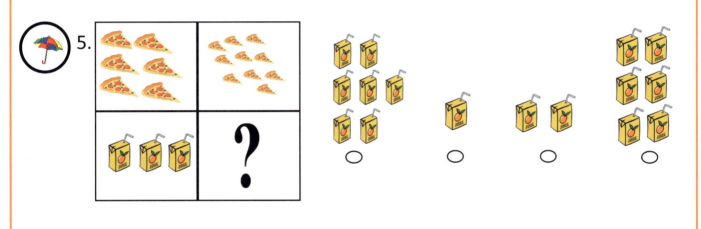

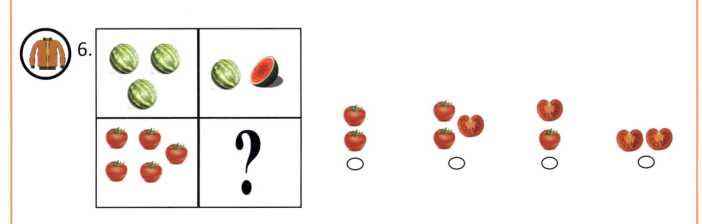

Number Analogies

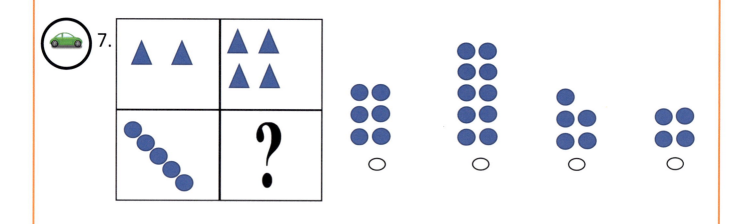

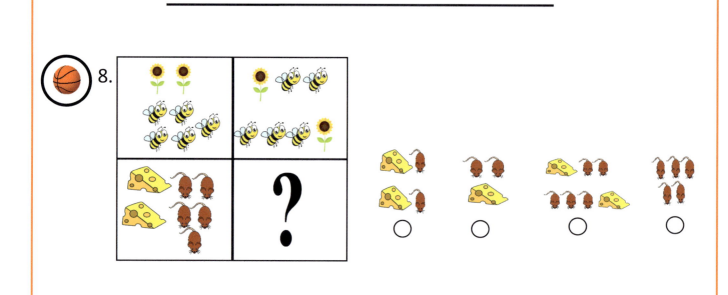

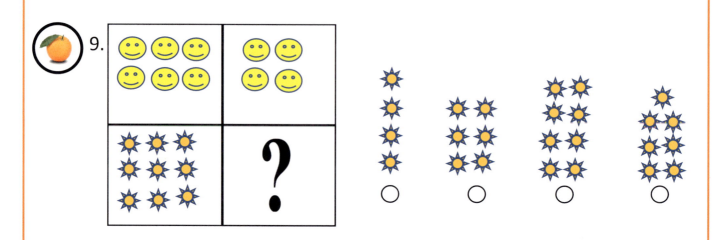

50

Number Analogies

10.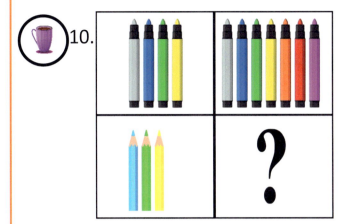

11.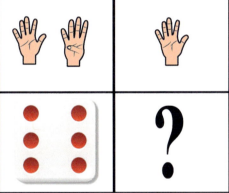

12.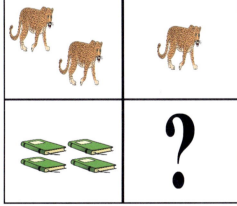

© Redmond Ridge Montessori

Number Analogies

13.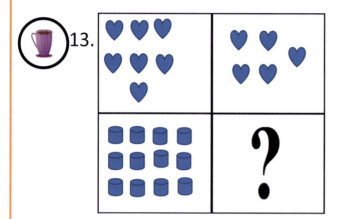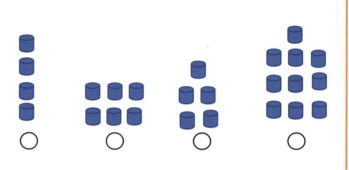

14.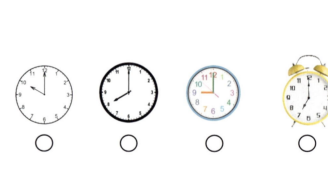

15.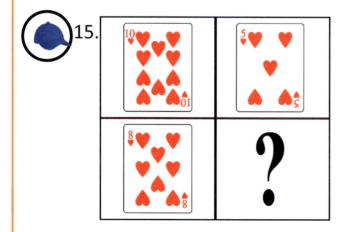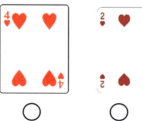

© Redmond Ridge Montessori

Number Analogies

16.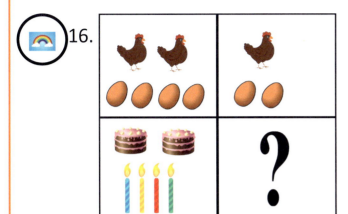

Section 3: Quantitative | Number Series

Students have to find the missing abacus rod that will complete the pattern.

1.

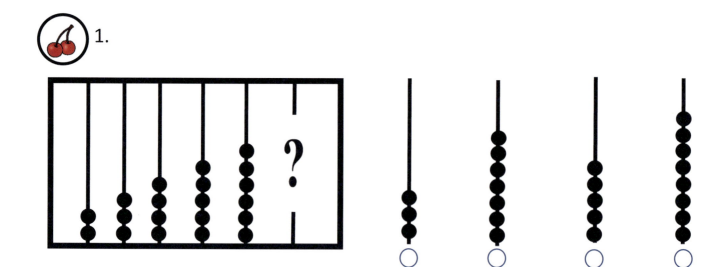

2.

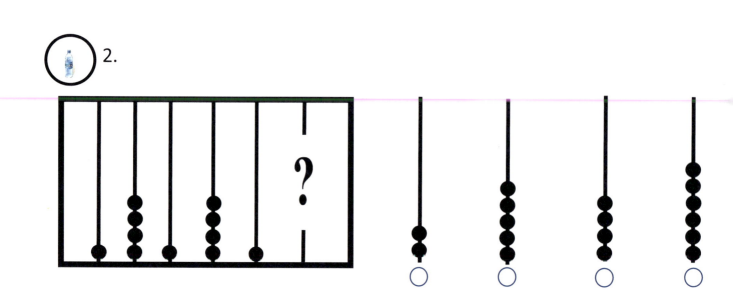

© Redmond Ridge Montessori

Number Series

 3.

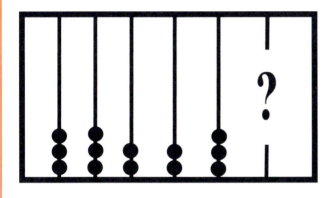    

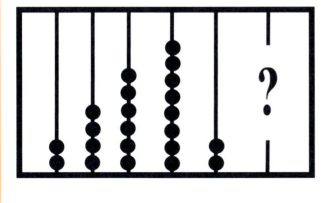 4.

Number Series

 5.

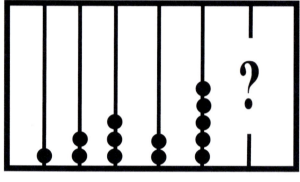    

 6.

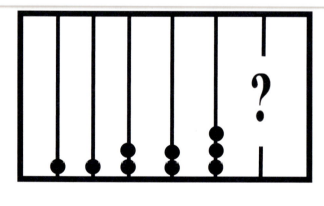   

Number Series

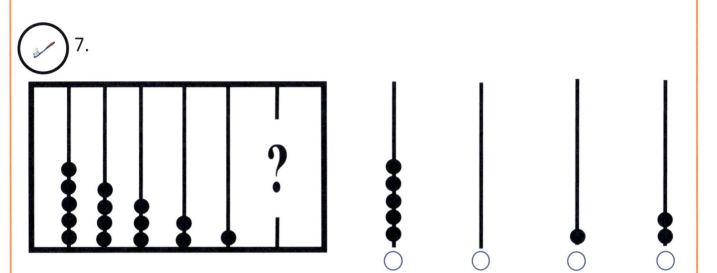

57

Number Series

 9.

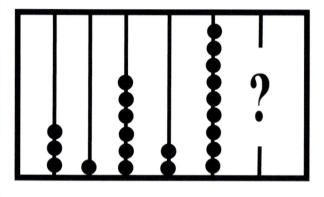    

 10.

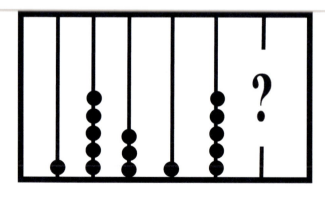    

Number Series

 11.

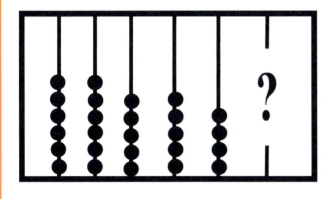    

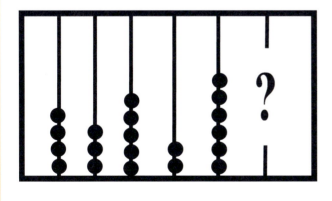 12.

Number Series

 13.

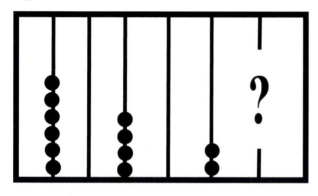 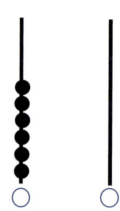 

 14.

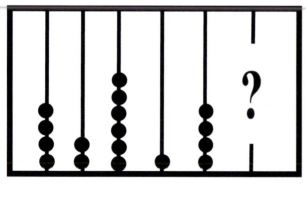 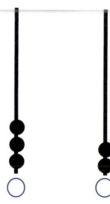 

© Redmond Ridge Montessori

Number Series

 15.

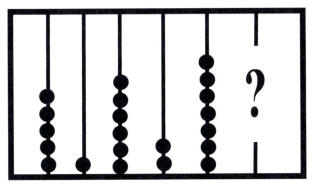    

 16.

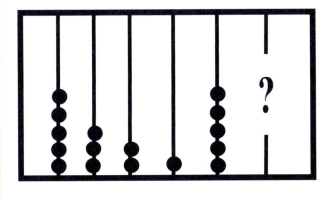   

Section 3: Quantitative | Number Puzzles

In this section there will be two trains. The train on the left must have the same total number of things as train on the right. Kids have to count the total number of things. The trains may have same or different number of cars attached to them and some might be empty as well. Students have to replace the train car that has question mark with the car from the options given that can balance the total number of things on both the trains.

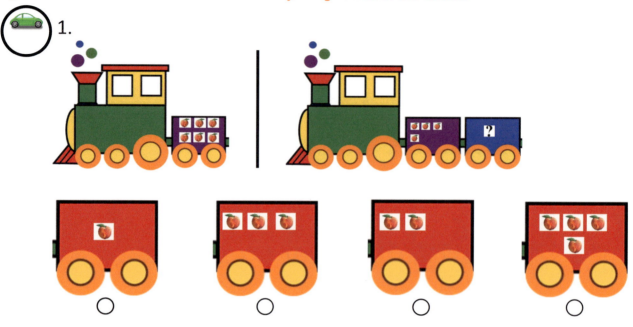

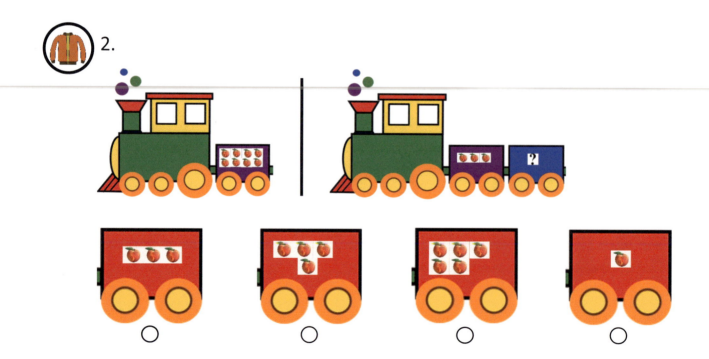

© Redmond Ridge Montessori

62

Number Puzzles

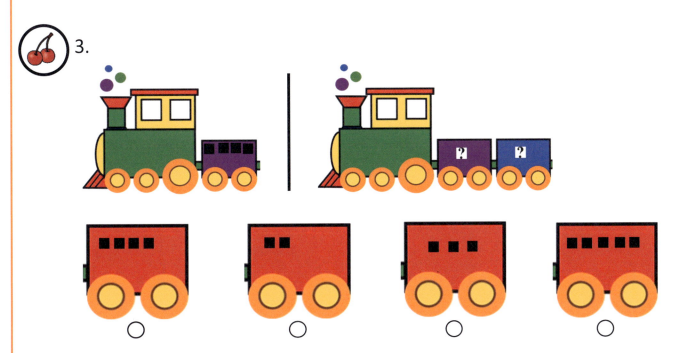

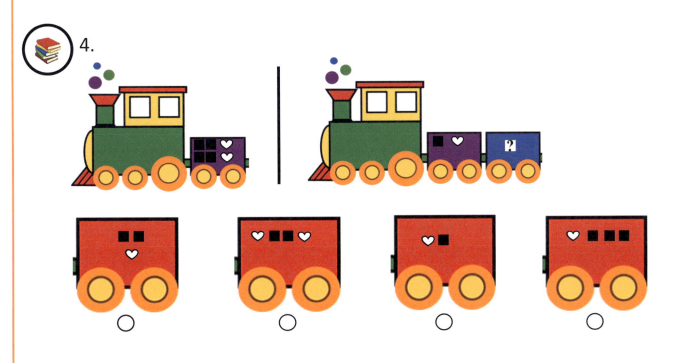

Number Puzzles

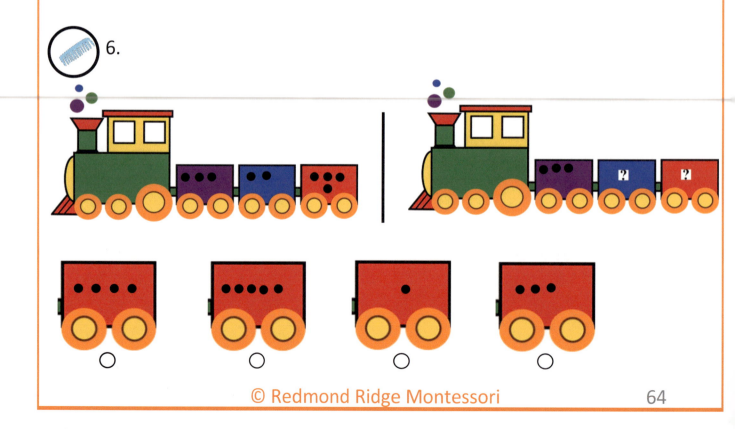

Number Puzzles

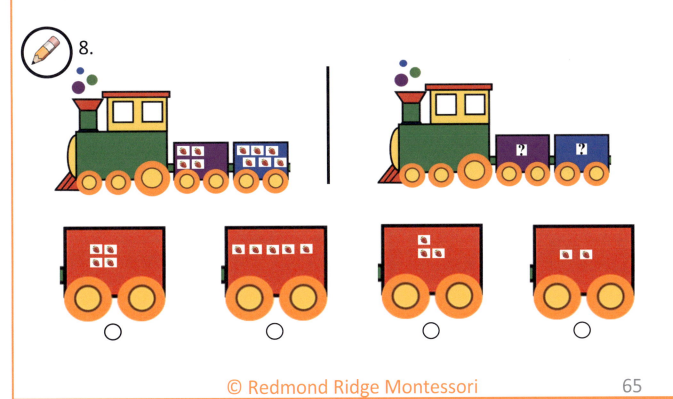

Number Puzzles

9.

10.

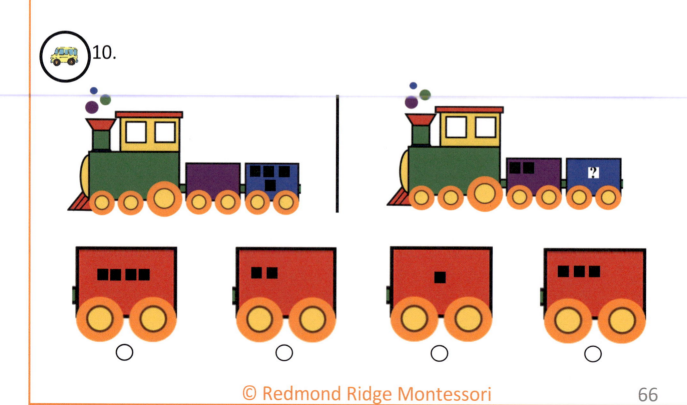

Number Puzzles

Number Puzzles

Answer Key - Verbal

Picture Analogies

1. B (Pig to piglet, duck to duckling)
2. A (Peach and banana are fruits, Broccoli and carrot are vegetables)
3. D (Penny = 1, Quarter = 25)
4. B (Refrigerator belongs in kitchen, bed belongs in the bedroom)
5. B (Airplane and bird are in sky, car and tiger are on land)
6. B (Horse and Bear are mammals, Alligator and Snake are reptiles)
7. C (Cookie is circle, Pizza slice is Triangle)
8. D (Omelet is made from egg, Cheese is made from milk)
9. A (Elephant's foot and person's foot)
10. C (Rectangle has 4 slides, Hexagon has 6 sides)
11. A (Orange juice is made from oranges, ketchup is made from tomatoes)
12. C (Money goes in a piggy bank, mail goes in a mail box)
13. A (Caterpillar grows into a butterfly, tadpole grows into a frog)
14. D (Sun to sunflower, basket to basketball)
15. C (Open book, closed book. Open box closed box)
16. B (Battery goes in flashlight, record goes in gramophone)

Picture Classification

1. C, Summer things)
2. B, Cubes)
3. C, Related to water)
4. D, 2D shapes)
5. B, Person doing some sport)
6. D, Uppercase vowels)
7. C, Wild animals)
8. D, Parts of plant)
9. C, Clocks)
10. D, Starts with the sound "f".
11. B, Living things.
12. C, Even numbers.
13. A, Farm animals.
14. B, Coloring materials.
15. C, Bags.
16. A, Camping things.

Sentence Completion

1. D	7. A, Ancient airplane.	12. C
2. C	8. B	13. D
3. D	9. B, Eiffel Tower.	14. A
4. B	10. A	15. B
5. A	11. B	16. A
6. D		

Answer Key – Non Verbal

Figure Analogies

1. C (Rotates clockwise)
2. C (1 less arrowhead, same pattern)
3. C (1 less outer hexagon)
4. B (Same shape with color swapped)
5. A (Flipped images)
6. C (Flipped and one less)
7. B (Double and connected)
8. B (Plus 1 line)
9. D (Rotated 90 deg clockwise)
10. A (Mirror image, color swapped)
11. B (Vertical and diagonal line)
12. C (Flipped and one small shaped added)
13. B (Mirror image)
14. C (Only horizontal shape left)
15. A (Rotated 90 deg counter-clockwise and small shape moved to front, same pattern)
16. B (Shape and color swapped)

Figure Classification

1. B (Triangles)
2. C (White shapes with black circle inside)
3. D (Blue outer square with white square inside and a different black shape)
4. D (White outer square with 2 same yellow colored shapes and different blue shape)
5. C (Same pattern)
6. D (Arrow pointing up)
7. A (4 sided shapes)
8. A (3 different shapes, only 1 is colored)
9. B (Shapes with symmetrical line)
10. D (Same pattern)
11. C (3 black squares)
12. C (Black shape with right point white arrow)
13. A (White shapes with black circle on middle of sides)
14. B (2 shapes, 1 is black and 1 is white)
15. D (2 black hearts, 2 other same white shapes)
16. D (Black arrow pointing towards a white star)

Paper Folding

1. D	7. A	
2. B	8. A	13. A
3. D	9. C	14. C
4. A	10. D	
5. C	11. D	
6. C	12. C	

© Redmond Ridge Montessori

Answer Key – Quantitative

Number Analogies

1. C (Adding 1)
2. D (Subtracting 3)
3. B (Subtracting 3)
4. C (Half)
5. A (Add 4)
6. B (Half)
7. B (Double)
8. C (Same)
9. D (Subtracting 2)
10. B (Adding 3)
11. B (Subtracting 4)
12. B (Half)
13. D (Subtracting 2)
14. B (Add 2)
15. A (Half)
16. B (Half)

Number Series

1. B (Increase by 1)
2. C (1,4,1,4,1,4)
3. A (3,3,2,2,3,3)
4. B (2,4,6,8, 2,4)
5. D (Pattern of 1,3,5 with 2 in between)
6. A (1,1,2,2,3,3)
7. B (Decrease by 1)
8. A (Repeat of pattern 4,1,3,2)
9. D (Rods 1,3,5 increase by 3 and Rods 2,4,6 increase by 1)
10. B (1,5,3,1,5,3)
11. A (6,6,5,5,4,4)
12. D (Rods 1,3,5 increase by 1 and Rods 2,4,6 decrease by 1)
13. B (Rods 1,3,5 decrease by 2, rods 2,4,6 are zero)
14. B (4,2,6,1,4,2,6,1)
15. D (Rods 1,3,5 increase by 1 and Rods 2,4,6 increase by 1)
16. A (5,3,2,1,5,3)

Number Puzzles

1. C	7. A	
2. C	8. B	13. D
3. B	9. B	14. A
4. D	10. B	
5. A	11. C	
6. D	12. A	

© Redmond Ridge MONTESSORI

Made in United States
Troutdale, OR
12/03/2023

15264659R00043